EVEN SUPERHEROES NEED HELP SOMETIMES

(Escaping The Minimum Mindset)

WILLIAM V. FIELDS

I dedicate this book to John Harriel of 2nd Call a true hero in the community whose life goal is to provide financial independence amongst his peers. Secondly, this book is dedicated to all the community activist behind the scenes making changes that they never truly get credit for. Thank You.

Table of Contents

Forward 1

Chapter 1
Know Yourself 3

Chapter 2
Check your Ego (Code Switching) 10

Chapter 3
Networking (And what it really means for you) 17

Chapter 4
How to Keep What You Have Once You Have It 25

Chapter 5
Living Below Your Means 37

Chapter 6
The Company You Keep 43

Chapter 7
Giving Back 46

Forward

After serving a 7-year sentence in prison for attempted murder, I was paroled on October 28, 2007. Like most individuals in my situation, this was the end of one chapter and the beginning of another.

Now that I was released, I found confusion swirled in my mind, *"What direction will I take my life now?"* and *"What's next?"* top the list of never-ending questions I played volleyball within my mind.

It's no secret, career options for parolees can be scarce; that might be putting it a bit too lightly. Sure, there are plenty of jobs that an ex-felon or parolee can find with minimum effort, but those likely aren't careers. Minimum effort equals minimum outcome. In fact, in my mind, minimum is a word that holds a lot of weight for someone's future. Webster defines minimum as the least quantity assignable, admissible, or possible. The lowest degree. When deciding to take the minimum is best approach, I always remind people that when a minimum path is chosen, a minimum job follows, minimum options soon follow and soon your future and the future of your family is a representation of the minimum choices you've made.

Minimum isn't for those looking to maximize.

If I'm being completely honest, the mentality of most ex-felons involves a false sense of confidence, which is usually generated from the value placed on possessions and what they can do to care for or impress others. As I've found, thinking with a mindset of minimum is the main recipe for disaster. Not only does it provide a breeding ground for mediocrity in everything you do, but it also directly affects the decisions you make. Let's face it, when someone's decisions begin to weaken, they also tend to straddle the fence between old behavior and their desire for a new life, which can eventually produce old results like drug dependency, alcoholism and reckless spending, to name a few. Soon, they are staring directly in the face of a ripple effect cycle of recidivism, or the tendency of a criminal to reoffend.

As humans, we are prone to assimilation. What does it mean to assimilate? By Merriam Webster, assimilate means to "cause (something) to resemble; liken". In other words, we tend to liken themselves as their actions to what they are familiar, comfortable or in the vicinity of. Admittedly, this can be both a good and bad thing. However, in the case of a felony mindset, assimilation of a bad behavior can often cause them to resort back to the street and hustle life, which placed them in prison to begin with - whether that's drugs, getting on government assistance or victimizing women in the community by leaching. This is another prime example of how thinking, surrounding yourself with and accepting minimum mindset can lead to your mind playing tricks on you in the form of the deadliest trap: confusing movement with progress. (Don't worry, we'll touch on that topic later in the book.) Whatever you must do to shake the minimum mindset, do it.

In this guide, we'll focus on the very real (but often dismissed) turmoil that some have faced (and are still facing) that has left them with a lack of skill to compete in the current and future work arena.

Buckle up! We're on a one-way trip away from the minimum mindset station. Next stop? Prosperity, fruitfulness and change!

Chapter 1
Know Yourself

Having direction is truly the key to making the move away from an immobile state, where you're continually spinning your wheels, towards progressive change. One of the greatest myths that people have is that they tend to confuse movement with progress. This couldn't be any more wrong if it tried to be. Having a lot of things to do every day with no clear goal of moving forward is not only just wasted time, it's a frequent mistake I see people make.

For example: if your goal is to own a house within five years you don't start your day with pointless errands like running the homies around to take care of their business or babysitting other people's kids. No, this starts the normalization of telling yourself that their business is why you couldn't take care of your own. People subconsciously destroy themselves without even knowing it by putting up roadblocks to their own success by playing the victim to other people's wants and needs. This behavior will consistently keep you stagnant for years. One of the only ways to combat this is to have an agenda written out, that serves as your daily personal guide, until it becomes your habit and no room for deviation is possible. Furthermore, if people really say they love you and want the best for you, they should understand your need to focus on yourself before you can be of any help to them. Keep in mind that a lot of us- myself included- have been programmed to align with certain belief systems and customs that harm us when it comes to socializing with other people. Because of this fact, reprogramming via new knowledge (i.e. reading and researching what you don't know) is a must.

Here is an example of what your daily agenda could look like:

6:00 am - read for an hour.

7:00 am - Get some form of exercise in. *If you can afford a gym membership, go there. If not, find other ways (walking around your neighborhood, outside workouts, etc.).*

Note: Exercise is vital to your success because if you look good most likely you will feel better People tend to hire healthy-looking people because it sends out the message this person is dependable and cares about their appearance. Remember: you are selling yourself every day; when you look good and feel good others will pick up on that energy too. Also, exercise teaches you discipline, which most incarcerated people can relate to, since exercise programs are mandatory on most prison yards.

8:00 am Go to work or school.

Note: Depending on if you are in school or working your agenda will vary. Let's say you are in school, once your school day is complete you should be at the library finishing up your homework for the week; once that is complete then focus on being a help to others if you please. If you are working, your goal after your workday is finished, should be to seek mentorship on how to advance in your current work position. A typical school or workday consists of eight hours, so from 8 am to 4pm you're either in class refining or working your job Monday through Friday.

9pm to 10pm most people are bringing their day to a close unless you are working night shifts. Although it seems mundane you are in your refining stage preparing physically and mentally for the grind. Liken it to a marathon runner they don't condition themselves attempting to run 10 miles on their first try out the gate. It is a slow build up to them getting the mental strength, leg strength, and cardiovascular strength as well as proper diet that will maintain them as they go further distances. Like it or not without proper refining you will fail continually until you decide to settle for less or just give up completely. You will fall on your face so create a routine you can follow through with so that you can condition yourself for success. Anyone can apply for a race just like a job, but without preparation you will fail falling by the wayside. Success can be exhausting butt with constant training you can condition yourself for progress.

So, Monday through Friday you have followed the agenda now the weekend is upon you and your schedule is somewhat free, right? Your weekend agenda should be solely focused on your next step, which brings us to knowing yourself.

I vividly remember sitting in Manchester park on August 3, 2000 blue Roca wear jeans, orange initial belt with matching orange LA hat and chucks with blue laces watching all my homies and homegirls enjoying the set day thinking to myself is this it, I mean really this is what my life will be I felt a void that wasn't being filled. I knew I could do better I just didn't know how to go about doing it. I had reached the pinnacle of Gang life I had a solid reputation, plenty of females, money, cars, jewelry, and could pretty much do whatever I wanted and yet I felt empty like the liquor bottles laying on the dead grass that circled the park in patches. There were only two more options left for me at that point prison or death. Shortly thereafter option one was set in motion when I was arrested for three attempted murders on some rivals. So, you can see that without direction life can get away from you quickly. Knowing who you are is critical to your development in life because it gives you a starting point to navigate from without it is far too easy to wander aimlessly from one situation to the next and allow unnecessary decisions and people to create chaos in your life who knowingly and unknowingly hold you back.

I knew at 19 years old that I wanted better, but lack of preparation and not understanding life doomed me to old habits that lead to my temporary downfall, this is a prime example of succumbing to habits and routines. Lesson to be learned from this is if you are going to succumb to your habits in life let them be good ones that help you rather then bad ones that hold you back and set you up for failure. Knowing yourself is also knowing your weaknesses for these are areas in which you can build and prepare yourself for when you come across things, people, are situations that you may not be astute. In correlation knowing your strengths gives you a compass to thrive in situations that bring you success and in doing so you may run across people who are strong in areas you are weak in and vice versa. In these types of conditions, it is critical to feed off one another, as they say steel sharpens steel.

While speaking at various career events and youth facilities I was taken aback by the lack of basic job etiquette that individuals lacked. This lack of understanding was so prevalent that I felt compelled to write this book as a guide for career awareness as well as stability. I found that most individuals fell into two categories: Thinkers and Workers.

It's my belief that people are born with gifts from birth - some have mental gifts, others have physical gifts, and few have both. From a young age, most people know which category they fall into or they can see it in others. This understanding makes them realize either their dominance in certain areas of their lives or lack thereof. Environment plays a part in this as well. It's a fact that certain environments aide in drawing out natural abilities while others stifle them. Unfortunately, most inner-city individuals start with the latter: no father, young mother, or generational ignorance.

No matter what people say there is a difference when a child is raised in a two-parent home versus a single parent home. Think about it as a home of educated parents versus non-educated parents. Most children growing up in a single parent home with minimal education never really learn the importance of an education or the true benefit of taking education seriously until it's too late. These same children tend to start school later than others, putting them at an early disadvantage. Also, in most single-parent homes, the assumption is that the teacher/school will teach their children. This unfortunate thought-process is not only false but hinders progress before it can even happen. How? In most cases teachers teach effectively to children who have already been assimilated with some form of education. The child who has already been immersed in math, reading, and spelling skills prior to kindergarten are more likely to latch onto the process of learning than those who have not. Once a child has a bad educational (or lack of educational) experience it usually sticks and they find other ways to adapt for survival, which includes acting out with behavior problems as a means of articulation. Aside from behavior problems, some children get into sports to keep themselves occupied with a hope of someday becoming the next sports star, even though the miniscule percentage of people that ever "make it". If we fast-forward to adulthood, these same individuals tend to still struggle with basic education. For clarification, their struggle with basic education doesn't make them less intelligent; it just means they're victims of pre-programming.

Reality hits most people right around high school graduation or GED time; that's when they realize that they don't have a suitable plan for life. In the middle of trying to figure out a life plan, some of them have a child or one on the way; or they form some sort of addiction, which alienates them from career-climbing since the habit is stronger than the will for more. With little resources, young adults with children or an addiction are often forced to the streets. So how do you combat this? Retraining yourself religiously by reading books, which serve to uplift you as well as rewire a lot of the nonsense you have been taught through the years. Remember: You cannot rebuild a new structure with old blueprints. If you try to do something new with an old mindset or process, it will be the same structural problem with a new look which ends up being more detrimental because the harm is out of sight, out of mind. That's why it is vital to be honest with oneself on what areas in life need to be corrected and improved for true growth. During the rewriting process some will find it an easy transition; others will struggle depending on how much damage has been done by others to them over the years, resulting in low self-esteem or self-inflicted harm from years of drug use.

Nevertheless, you can rebuild if you have the desire. Just know we all struggle with learning new information and new ways of seeing and living life especially as adults.

My awakening came during my first year of incarceration when I start to read books regarding my history. This is when my eyes were finally opened, and I have always likened it to Neo in the Matrix. Soon, everything started to make sense, but it was also scary because I had to admit I had a lot of flaws that I had to overcome. The process was daunting and frustrating to say the least, but I knew I had to do better once I knew better. So, don't fret. The fact that you are reading this is fulfilling the first step towards changing your life and setting forward the plan that God has for you. Yes, even every set back can be used to forward you if you use it correctly. Think about it like this: you may as well earn a lesson from situations where you took a headache for free, right? Regardless of your start, you must pinpoint where your strengths lie and ask yourself are you a *Thinker* or *Worker* because this can greatly affect how well you do in your future career.

If you are a thinker you should focus on a career that will allow you to grow and eventually own your own business such as customer service, law, or social service. These jobs require comprehension skills, writing, and socializing with different types of people.

If you are more of a worker consider getting a trade where you can use your physical skills to build and create such as electrical, plumbing, and wielding. These professions allow for business ownership once you have completed an apprenticeship.

In short: find your fit and be the best at whatever you decide to do. As for myself I was fortunate to possess both qualities of worker and thinker. Being incarcerated for six years gave me a lot of time to think, read, and workout and most would say what else would you do? My answer absolutely nothing everyday decisions are optional I could have done like most inmates and just let the time do me playing games, telling war stories, and getting high, but instead I decided to really analyze how I had gotten that point in my life so I studied those around me and read a plethora of books on self-improvement, social development, and psychology. I totally remolded myself and how I viewed life as well as where I put my energy. I realized that I was a natural leader I just had been leading people in the wrong direction as well as myself. I knew if I put as much energy into gangbanging into building myself, I could be whatever I wanted to be and great at doing it. Initially I went to college to become an inside wireman, but fate would have it, I became a Journeyman Lineman a career that I truly love. I currently Own a home and two apartment buildings which isn't bad for a kid who grew up in apartments his entire life and yet I want more because I know I can do more. Too most this is incredible, but there are numerous stories like mine you just must be conscience of them and believe in yourself foremost. I am one of many, so I don't see myself as anything special I'm just a guy who knew he could always have what he wanted if he put his mind to it. In my youth I was just misguided and lazy I wanted everything to just fall in my lap it took for me to go to prison to realize I needed to just simply grow up.

Chapter 2

Check Your Ego (Code Switching)

As I mentioned in the first chapter, most ex-felons (myself included) grew up in environments that operated on a different set of rules then what the average person in the job arena operates off.

One of the biggest difficulties that I had when I paroled and enrolled in college was dealing with societies set of rules versus prison, gang, and ghetto rules. Street/ prison rules evolve around a person's word, speech tone, and body language. At its core you are only as good as your word and type of reputation you have. When you are known for having a solid word you can move amongst others in the life with currency called respect; with this respect you are entrusted with viable information and resources and are able to make a living based on your connections acquired by street cred.

The dilemma comes when transitioning into the regular work force because they don't care about your street cred, who you may be in your other life or the sense of value you place in a person having a solid word. Most supervisors or co-workers will talk to you in a very condescending way, expecting for you to just take it as a form of instruction, without any fear in the way they speak to you. In the streets this type of posturing could end violently, but in the workforce, it must be ignored in order to elevate to the next level.

There's a valuable platitude that I was told while going through my transition "An idiot is going to get their issue you don't have to be the one to give it to them". Before applying this statement to my life, I allowed myself to get out of character and check one of my college instructors in an aggressive manner; after doing so I felt no real sense of relief. It didn't solve the problem and made the situation worse because it made me seem out of control to the other instructors whose opinion mattered to me. The result of me lashing out was entertainment for fellow classmates, a hostile learning environment in the lab, and a sit down with me and the other instructors that yielded nothing more than me looking out of control.

The caveat that you should gather from my shortcoming in that situation is that rudeness is the weak man's interpretation of strength. When you are confident in yourself and know where you come from, it's asinine to let a square throw you off your focus. Be sure that you learn from every situation and shortcoming that you encounter, because you will come up short a lot in your new life, but it's all part of the growth process. Everyone successful person has had some form of struggle that they went through before they reached their goal, so don't fall into a depression if you fail a test or don't understand something. Push your ego to the side and learn to ask for help before you start to give yourself a pity party and making excuses to quit before you even begin. These setbacks will only be strengthening you for future hurdles you may face. Keep in mind it's all a conditioning phase, like fighting in the streets. Some individuals have natural abilities while others had to develop their hands from wins and losses. But look back, the better your hand got, the less fights you probably found yourself in, correct? The same laws apply to learning. The better you become at solving problems, the less they become actual problems; I guarantee you of this.

In hindsight, there were a lot of opportunities in my life where I could have thrown in the towel and given up when I was faced with adversity. Trying to get my class A driver's license was one case.

Living in the Los Angeles there was never a need to learn how to drive a stick shift vehicle. I mean, everyone I knew owned an automatic, so learning how to drive stick wasn't necessary. The first truck driving school was in the city of Fontana and they charged $750 per person to teach people how to drive big rig trucks. There were two instructors, one spoke entirely Spanish and the other was twenty-one years old with a cocky attitude and no true desire to teach. So, the students basically lined up and taught each other, which was very frustrating, I could never really get a full grasp on the technique that way. I got fed up with this pointless endeavor and quit with no refund in the deal. I had saved that money for months and wanted to burn the school down for keeping my money when they didn't keep their end of the deal. In my street mentality they had worked me out of my money, but I knew I had to take it on the chin. I knew that the next time I would survey the class before I handed over my money to make sure I was getting what I paid for. I admit that it was hard to move on from, but I did. I've learned over the years that failure can never be an option and nothing great comes in one try.

A few months later I was stationed in the desert working a transmission job and found another truck company in the next town, fortunately for me (having learned from the first experience) I passed on this school before giving up my money. I eventually found a school for $800 in Rialto. The school only had one instructor and I was able to learn within a day how to drive a stick and back the truck up in the various positions necessary to pass the DMV's class A test. The test consisted of three parts: the written, which you must take before actually getting behind the wheel, a walk around, where you must verbally identify parts on the truck as well as their functions plus other parts on the truck interior as well as exterior. The third part consists of the actual driving part, which you and the instructor go on a fifteen minute drive from the DMV parking lot on the streets around the neighborhood and onto the freeway and back where you are tested on your shifting of gears, lane changing, and braking. My first go I failed before I even made it to the driving portion I had forgotten one of the parts on the interior and it was an instant fail, which means I had to come back again to restart the entire process again. On the second day I got everything on the walk around correct, so it was on to the driving portion of the test, which took me around a course the

DMV sets up with three mistakes given before you fail. I failed that portion too, so I had one more chance to nail it the next day. If I didn't, I would have to pay the school another $800 to retake the test again. That night I prayed for strength to be at my best. My instructor was a Christian lady whose name I can't recall now, but what I can tell you is that she was a living angel. As soon as the drive started, she began telling me about which church she attended and where she grew up; this instantly put me at ease and I no longer viewed my drive as a test, but just a regular drive. Before I knew it, we were done with the test and was walking into the DMV with my completion form! What a blessing. I felt elation that only comes upon a person a few times in their life for I knew God had shined his light on me that day specifically. Seriously my back was against the wall, but I kept the faith through it all and came out victorious none-the-less. I had to put my ego aside and ask for help in this situation, but let's take another look at how ego can deter your path.

As a youth I enjoyed learning new things about my environment as well as educationally, but as I grew older, I started to question the purpose of getting a formal education. Around seventh grade I had begun to have a disdain for school mostly because I didn't see anyone around me benefiting from attending school. Getting a diploma was simply a means to keep my mother off my back. The reality? Growing up in South Central Los Angeles, I didn't think I would live past 21 years old so why waste time doing something I didn't enjoy? I was (and still am) a very rebellious person on certain belief systems. My ego at the time had me convinced that I didn't need school education for my mental and personal development; sadly, I was wrong. I attended over five different high schools before finally graduating. I didn't attend prom or any type of school activities growing up, which meant I missed out on countless valuable memories and lifelong friendships that could have been spawned from a little participation.

My ego told me back then that if I could count money, I was good. Even that proved to be wrong. I really had no concept of what money was or what constituted poverty from wealth. In my adolescent frame of mind,

I associated doing well with new clothes, cars, and jewelry, which could easily be attained by selling drugs or robbing people, so that's what I did to get by in my teenage and early adult years. Having a false sense of self-importance caused me to venture down a path that would ultimately lead to me losing myself in a pursuit to create the type of world where I called the shots and wouldn't be controlled by society's rules.

Thus my alter ego manifested baby Tr3y Devil, an ego-driven individual who acted on all impulses without thought for others or the environment that surrounded me. I played by my own rules without much regard for anything else. My aspiration of wealth at the time was having an apartment and paying rent to someone else. I deemed houses and mortgage payments for professionals who were smarter than I was and who grew up in good homes. I was so wrong and ignorant back then, all because I let my ego feed my insecurities and lack of discipline.

So many times, in my adult life I have reflected on my past and said to myself if I only knew what I know now I would have never sold myself so cheap. All the money I've gone through I could've owned multiple homes and investments but having no discipline at the time and true education I played the fool pretending to be a prince. Don't sell yourself cheap ever in life. Never be afraid of the unknown by accepting falsehoods of what you can and can't be in this life.

For whatever you put your time, energy, and focus into you will see those fruits.

Let me ask you something: how many real niggas do you know? From my observation "nigga" is no longer a label attributed to just black people, but a mindset of rebellion against society that anyone can cling to. Take notice of what this mentality is producing in your life. I promise you to be a real nigga at 35 to 45 doesn't hold as much potency when you look back on your life and all your children are struggling and repeating your same mistakes and all you can do to mask the pain is getting blunts, cigarettes, and alcohol in your system.

I often get asked a lot when I go out and speak to various groups was prison hard or do, I regret going and my answer is always surprising to them. I feel like going to prison was the best thing that happened to me. I was incarcerated at 20 years old in 2001 and didn't parole until 2007 at the age of 26. Going to prison allowed me to refined William Fields again and develop him properly. Prison took me away from all the distractions the world had to offer and gave me some much-needed time to reflect on the direction I needed to go in. Having time to think, I was suddenly able to reflect on how my decisions all led me to that point. I realized that for me to truly change I had to break away from all the belief systems that caused me harm. In order to do this, I meditated and took rap music out of my daily program so that I could rebuild on uninfluenced ground. In its place I started to plant knowledge from various books. Over time I started to feel an internal change and how I not only viewed myself, but others and how I handled certain situations. I thought more and reacted less which started to bring me an inner peace that was void before. The most challenging thing to come from this metamorphosis was having to adhere to gang beliefs I no longer believed in. Coming into the system under my flag I still had to perform for the gang at times, even when it didn't even make sense to me. I didn't hate other black people anymore, yet I still attacked them due to my gang affiliations. When possible, I tried to handle situations with decorum whereas I would have used violence in the past. These were all practice in breaking down my ego. The ironic thing is that often, I didn't even know I was preparing for a far greater challenge that would meet me upon my release. Now, society faced William and not Tr3y Devil. Tr3y Devil was submerging more and more as the years went by and soon, William emerged. William was far stronger because he could take criticism and had no fear of failing; after all, he had failed his entire life and was still breathing. With each accomplishment he grew stronger with self-knowledge, which he'd gleaned through his reading and enduring while applying the lessons from life that he'd learned.

One recurring lesson that stayed with me during this phase was just how much a person must first be shoved in dirt before it can become a flower that grows. To do this, your ego must first be in check because where your ego is, is also where your destination is. Making decisions based on an elevated ego will cause you to make rash, impromptu decisions based off old past behaviors. Don't do it. Choose better. Choose to deflate ego in order to inflate your direction.

Chapter 3

Networking
(And what it really means for you)

One of the key elements in any business paradigm or self-help program will imply the need to network with others to find success. Still, like so many words and catch phrases that are thrown around, networking can be lost in translation, according to life experiences.

Where I grew up networking was defined as the ability to acquire drugs, guns, or other goods at a lower price from my homies so that I could make more of a profit or get things my homies simply didn't have. Often that meant doing business with rival sets or other races to accomplish these goals. Fortunately, I realized early on that, at its core, the gang life wasn't about colors, but about money. Simply put, if it doesn't make dollars it didn't make sense. It can be easy to get caught up in the smoke and mirrors of the street or political arena, with all its distractions of racism, policies, and beliefs. Little do some know, though, there are people that understand the game and are making money with those that can turn a profit- regardless of race, color or gender. When money is being made, only the people on the losing side take up the torch for some form of distraction, simply because they have nothing else to do but to create confusion. Think about it: it's always the person with the least to lose and the most to gain (i.e. the broke person) that wants to protest making money by any means. Rarely do I ever see productive people complaining openly about issues, because they're too busy making moves. As I've become more seasoned, I've quickly learned that making money and connections supersedes a lot of the nonsense I was told over the years. Soon, networking became a form of maturity in my life. As my vision changed, I saw men as men. In my mind, skin color and gang affiliation became secondary once currency was being made. Currency building allowed for relationship-building, which in turn tore down mental walls I had built for my life.

As you've probably noticed by now, I'm huge on using real life examples. Why? Easy. Personally, I know that I find it extremely hard to take advice from anyone if I don't have any evidence that they have personal experience with what they're talking to me about. If they're giving me secondhand knowledge, how can I be sure what they are saying is copasetic are even authentic when it sounds contrived humdrum in its flow? It's like a person telling you how to be successful and stay the course when they have been given every tool in life to succeed from birth. How can a person like this truly relate to a person coming from a single parent home or drug addicted parents? Unless they have had first-hand experience, they can't. And no, a textbook can't ever educate you over experience. Relatability is not a vicarious luxury that one can simply tap into.

So, I am captivated equally by someone's successes and their failures, because either can guide you in a path rather quickly. Furthermore, I like to debunk excuses people tend to use as to why they are not successful or cannot acquire a lifestyle. If you were to interview ten gangbangers from various gangs, they would probably all have similar stories on how they came from a bad community, single parent homes, drugs, and violence. The same would hold true if you interviewed ten millionaires and asked them what the key to their success was. The likelihood that you'd hear discipline, goals, dedication, hard work, etc., is high. Remember: the only variation between the story of the unsuccessful and the successful person's story is what decisions they made when faced with difficult situations in their lives.

In the streets, people tend to deal with you according to your stripes and reputation. When it comes to networking, try looking at it from the perspective of earning stripes to negotiate with later. You could be gone from the streets for years, but because of your stripes (networking) people will show you love in the form of currency, favors, or information that leads you in the direction of a win. Consistency, reliability, and decency will take you a long way in life if you give it a try.

I was about two to three years into my six-year sentence when I met Dr. Ranford Reece in group put together by the Incarcerated Youth Program (IYO) within the prison library. By then I had a couple of books under my belt, making my mind sharp and aware. There were about 20 inmates in the group that day, so the energy was mixed. Less than half of the class was there to learn, another group was just tired of sitting in their cell; the remainder just wanted to stare at the supervisor of the IYO programs daughters' shapely butt. After hearing Dr. Reece speak, I was enamored neither not by his title or football stats, but how he rebounded from the complete failure of a lifelong dream. You see, he grew up in the south in a small town with a father who was a local sportscaster and his entire life was centered on going to the NFL. I strongly empathized with how he had to leave his town because it was a constant reminder of him not making his dream. I know firsthand what an unaccomplished dream looks and feels like and can do to a person over time if that void is not filled. So, to hear how he was able to rise out of that depression and carve an entirely new course for his life set a fire under me to continue my journey. Regardless of the fact that I had no idea what my actual purpose was, I knew that I would be the best at whatever I decided to do because, just like Reese, I was going to have to start from scratch once I paroled.

Once Reese bared his soul at the IYO session, he left his contact information on the board and I quickly jotted it down, because I knew this was a networking opportunity I needed to jump on. As all the inmates filed out of the library, Reese met us at the exit with a handshake, which left me with a sense of humanity I hadn't felt in a while. I was so used to be my alter ego that it felt strange to simply be a man conversing with another man. In that moment I wasn't an inmate, I wasn't Tr3y Devil...I was just William Fields.

I contacted Reese right away and he encouraged me to write the book I was working on at the time titled *House of Failure*. He even found me a couple of pen pals to correspond with in order to occupy my time. The last few years of my sentence we kept in constant contact as I continued to build so that I would be ready for the opportunities that Reese could provide.

On October 26, 2007, I paroled from Cantilena State Prison and instead of being picked up from the gates by my family I opted to take the Greyhound bus to the Downtown Los Angeles station. The main reason I wanted to take the Greyhound bus home was, so I could study my DMV pamphlet which my uncle Joe had sent me a few months before I paroled. I knew there was not much I could do without a driver's license or ID. The entire moment of arriving at the station and seeing my family was surreal. While I had read about the word "surreal" while being incarcerated, I never truly understood its meaning until that moment. I'd lost my parole date a few times and honestly didn't know the day would come. But here it was. As I embraced my mother Terri, and brother Corey, I realized that it was now time to put all my discipline to work.

Within a few days of my release I had my license and my California ID. My next move was to enroll in college and publish my first book *House of Failure,* which I'd completed from within the walls. Since I'd been busy taking courses in prison, I had a nice head start on getting my AA degree and felt confident about enrolling in my first real college. Mount Zack was a junior college to Cal Poly, and I was excited to take psychology. Although I didn't stay long (due to another opportunity that came my way - don't worry, I'll elaborate later) these were memorable moments in my decision to chase more.

I had been out for about two weeks when I reconnected with Reese again to participate in a video series, he had created called Prison Race, which followed the book of the same title. It was the first time I'd seen Reese face-to-face from our first encounter at CSP. The video went viral shortly after and the next thing I know I'm at the University of Southern

California (USC) giving lectures to the sociology department headed by one of Reese's undergrad professors, Dr. Jackson. He had seen my video as well and wanted me to come out and share my story. After my first lecture Dr. Jackson set up a lunch with me and the Dean of the sociology department at USC, DR. Flynn. So, there I was less than a month out of prison, having a lunch meeting with various professors about enrolling in USC. It was unbelievable to say the least. I went from being in a SHU program, to a prison mainline, to a restaurant at USC where the Dean was giving me an opportunity to be a student at one of the most prestigious universities in California. In just a short amount of time I was reaping the benefits from networking and establishing a relationship with people who were offering to help make me better, because they saw the drive in me.

I've come to realize over the years (and through numerous situations), that people will go over and beyond for you when they see you giving it all you must make it happen for yourself. In the same breath, I've seen opportunities arise for people that they weren't even looking for. Over the next few years I would continue to build consistent relationships with people, thus building a strong network of professionals that were only a phone call away. Still, my future was still in my hands. Yes, I had the connections, but they'd made their way in life and I was still in the building stages for my own as it unfolded. So, from 2007 to 2009 I was on my grind hard doing lectures about prison reform and my life at various colleges throughout southern California. I did a few radio interviews; spoke at juvenile facilities and I once was even featured on Time Warner with news reporter Jacqueline Toueg. That connection came through networking, too. I'd met Jaqueline through a sculptor at Los Angeles Trade-Tech College (LATTC) that read my book and referred me to her. This is yet another example of a good use of networking to further your net worth, purpose and endeavors.

As I mentioned earlier in the chapter, I attended Mount Zack temporarily before switching course and enrolling into LATTC. While serving my six years in prison, my uncle Joe stayed in contact with me the entire time. I looked forward to Uncle Joe's updates on current events, family, and the career climate. At my sentencing hearing he'd wisely advised me to make prison my college. I did as I was told and started crafting my body and mind to be strong for the challenges that would await me once I returned home. After all, six years is a long time to be away from society. When I was released so much had changed, including me. I was no longer angry, confused, or without purpose; I knew I would be great at whatever I put my mind to. Nothing was above or beneath me, if it led me to my goal of being an example to those I had led astray with my misguided and personal issues of grandeur. Up until then I had no clue of what I wanted to do outside of building a gang reputation which only yielded a prison sentence. Besides reading, writing, and doing college courses I took an electrical class provided by the prison. It gave me a sense of hope that I had some type of skill to fall back on. No pun intended, but it was as though the light came on.

Before I continue, I must say, there comes a time in your life when you must stop and analyze where your life is going. If you're a person who has no record and are between the ages of 16 and 20, I suggest you experiment with college and chasing uncertainty before you get dead set on a career path. On the other hand, if you are reading this and are unsure of what direction you want to go and are between the ages of 25 and 35, go get a trade while your body permits.

In my opinion, most college degrees are without merit financially unless you are going to become a doctor or an engineer. Frankly, it didn't make much sense to me to gather debt for a degree that would pay me $30,000 a year just to say I graduated from a prestigious university. Those titles become irrelevant when you are struggling day-to-day upon graduation. Decisions like these must be considered so that you don't move backwards on a quest at becoming more, doing more and acquiring more. At the time I had no debt or credit to my name and didn't have the leisure of wasted moves. I told myself that every move had to count and that applied to the food I put into my body, the people I hung around, the women I dated, and most importantly my career decisions.

So appealing as it was to take the Dean of USC up on her offer, I chose to pursue a trade at LATTC.

LATTC is in downtown Los Angeles and offers numerous trades to choose from - for whatever you think your niche might be. I chose to take electrical construction. So, there I was two months out attending LATTC, taking D/C theory to figure out ohms law, series circuits, parallel circuits, and combination circuits. To be completely honest, I was lost and had to stay after class every day to get tutoring in math because it had never been a strong suit of mine. At first, I didn't understand the equations, but it just took a lot of concentration for me to get it down the first few times; I had to grasp an understanding because failure wasn't an option. If I happened to fall short, I wanted to at least know I gave it a 100 percent - even if I had to retake the class. I barely passed those advanced courses, but I later became quite good after less pressure was applied. When I look back now, I know I put a lot on myself because I wanted to be great with every fiber in my being. While I was taking the electrical courses, I also took general classes to finish up my AA degree.

Over the next two years, a typical day for me would begin at 6 am end at 9 pm. While most of my peers only took the electrical classes, I took as many classes as I could and when I finished my general classes I went to the library to study and finish my homework. Before going home, I would stop by 24-Hour Fitness to exercise. This routine gave me a purpose every day and kept me away from the nonsense. At the end of 2009 I had successfully completed all my courses including a six-month climbing class, that had just been added to the list of trades LATTC, ran by retired lineman Ken Bushman. I met a lot of great guys in that class, but few stuck out to me, like Ryan Reed. Ryan Reed had an undeniable drive for greatness that paralleled my own and his story was the epitome of how staying focused and networking go hand and hand. Every year the Department of Water and Power holds a lineman rodeo, where different climbing schools and journeyman compete for awards. Everyone in my class wanted to enter, but few put in the extra effort to compete, including myself. Ryan went on to compete and was seen by recruiters from all utilities in the area. Ryan was a great climber and it didn't take long for him to catch the attention of many of the recruiters there. After graduation, my classmates and I all scattered out into the world looking for jobs in our chosen trade. The first written test we took was for the city of Burbank, which puts out a test every few years where hundreds apply mostly for one position. The written test is used to lower the number of applicants down to the few they want to interview. The final three included Ryan Reed. Unbeknownst to Ryan Reed, one of the same recruiters that was at the rodeo also sat on the interview panel. Shortly after Ryan Reed would be an apprentice at Burbank utility. Another example of networking at its finest. Also keep in mind even the strongest super heroes needed to team up to defeat certain foes as well as villains hence the Sinister Six, League of Doom, Justice League, and the Avengers at some point in your life you are going to need a team to overcome certain problems in your life.

Chapter 4

How to Keep What You Have Once You Have It

By now I hope you have gathered that your mindset is the key to unlocking your success. Yes, you will have setbacks, which you can't plan for, followed by confusion as you embark on this new journey for your life. If you don't allow these setbacks to hold you back, you will succeed at whatever you decide to do - that is a guarantee. In life there are certain fundamentals that are definite, such as the fact that the combination of discipline, persistence, and hard work will yield results no matter how far you are in life. The change begins and ends with you.

As a felon with attempted murder on my record, I've never let that label define me as a person or allowed it to become a handicap when it came time to find jobs or meet new people or territory. Too many times I have met people who allow their past to define their future. Thoughts such as *"I cannot get a particular job because they don't hire felons"* is at the top of this list. Most job interviewers make their decisions based on personal interactions with the person, which is the purpose for the job interview. The main quality most interviewers are looking for is compatibility between yourself and the organization.

Appearance is also key in this decision, because it can make or break you before you even open your mouth. In this society we have been brainwashed to believe that a suit and tie is the only way you can enter this platform, which is not true. The first thing you want to do is make sure you are wearing the appropriate outfit for the job, so definitely take the time to see how people dress in the position you are interviewing for and mold your attire after them. Think of it like this: a Crip going to join a Crip gang wearing all red. Model yourself after the environment you're walking into.

The biggest mistake most applicants make when applying for the **JATC** was wearing a suit for a construction job, which made them appear ignorant to the culture. A Journeyman Lineman's typical attire is a FR shirt, boots, and jeans. If the job is more casual- like an office position - shoot for clothes that fit your physique, not tight, but fits the way it should. Too often, I see guys go into interviews with suits they wear to church on Easter or a court date and it shows. Furthermore, designer haircuts, braids, and shabby beards must go too. This is an adjustment from the old to the new and you must really want it. Plainly put you must grow to grow.

There were times in your past when that was cool, but now is the time to decide what is more important: staying real or laying the foundation for your future? Don't let foolish pride or a drug habit stop your money. After all, when it is all said and done, and your money is right you can make all the personal statements you choose, but until then learn to play the game.

Another trait you must be aware of is posture and how you articulate yourself. Because of this, it's vital that you get with other likeminded people and do mock interviews. This will help tremendously because others will be able to critique you while your confidence builds. You can have the best intentions in the world, but if you can't articulate your thoughts, you will struggle and miss many opportunities. Listening to audiobooks while driving and repeating how they speak is good practice to help, too.

Some more common things people overlook are eye contact, a strong handshake, and having personality. Giving the employer eye contact is key, but too much eye contact can weird a person out, so do it when you initially meet and when you're making a point.

A nice firm handshake shows confidence and strength, so be sure to focus on that as well. Lastly, relax. You can do everything right, but if you come off as a robot it will show.

So, smile and have fun trying to make the interview as pleasant as possible. Your goal is to leave the interviewer with the feeling of *I wouldn't mind having that person around for 8 hours at a time every day*. Attitude is often better than skills because skills can be taught; attitude is often ingrained. A poor attitude shows a person's character; at the end of the day you can have great skills, but if you have a terrible attitude no one is going to want to work around you.

Fact: The greatest strength a person with nothing to lose has is hunger. When you're hungry you appreciate the smallest gestures and are willing to work harder than most, because you have been denied for so long. The problems occur when you start to see your strategies pay off and you get a few checks under your belt. It's at this moment that you begin the minimum thinking, which leads to being content with mediocrity. Soon, you're telling yourself things like *this job is cool, I could stay here I got a car, I'm paying my rent, plus I have going out money*. From this point on, you either stay past your prime or start to take the job for granted. This is when you begin using your phone during work hours, showing up late or lacking consistency. The attitude then becomes *I can always get another job I got this one*.

Enough is enough. Stop this type of thinking before it eats away at your potential. This type of thinking is not only selfish, but self-destructive. You should never burn bridges or forget those who helped you when you were down. Too many people only think about themselves instead of being a resource for others that are in need. Likewise, no matter what you do practice excellence and be the best; it doesn't matter if you're selling Jaguars or mattresses (which I did for a year before I started my apprenticeship).

Outside of having a relationship with God, selling mattresses helped me hone my attitude and people skills. Within my first three months of working at Sleep Train I had learned a variety of skills. From opening a store by myself, to running a cash register and approving people for loans, my knowledge on business and people grew leaps and bounds. It constantly took me out of my comfort zone by making me connect with a variety of personalities by the day. I was ten months in when I met Kevin Kessler and his wife at the Moreno Valley location. What caught my attention immediately was the drawing of a transforming bank on the back of his orange shirt.

When I inquired about it, he asked me how I knew what it was. I informed him that I went to college to become a Lineman, to which he replied, "then why are you working here?"

I told him I had been applying everywhere for positions and he asked if I'd tried the JATC.

I said was clueless what it was and asked for more information. He said it was the outside Lineman apprenticeship and that they were taking applications that month for interviews and I could go on the website to get further information. Once I got home that night, I went on JATC website to get all the information that I needed to apply for the position. After a week I had all my paperwork and required material submitted.

Up until that point I had failed the Edison written test twice and the Burbank test too. All the years that I'd taken my education for granted had handicapped me when it came time to take standardized tests. Still, it never detoured me from my dream; I knew God would take care of me as long as I did my part and didn't give up or start feeling sorry for myself. I knew if I could just get to the interview, I would get a spot as an apprentice. Why? Well, I had been working on my verbal and people skills the entire time I had been out and was great at getting my point across in a clear fashion. When I finally got word that I'd received an interview, I was ecstatic. The weeks leading up to the interview I practiced with all classmates doing mock interviews, secured a pair of work jeans, and an FR shirt with boots. I had everything ready to go. When the day arrived, the street was packed with diesel trucks in parking lots and on both sides of the narrow street of Limonite in Riverside, Ca. I managed to find a spot for my small Dodge Neon after circling the school for ten minutes. I'd arrived an hour early so I would have time to put my mind at ease and pray for the words to say. After thirty minutes I had my spiel down for the interviewers. Still, it didn't go as I planned.

When I walked into the JATC the ladies at the front desk had me take a seat on some couches near the door along with four other guys. With there being so many people being interviewed, the interviewers were getting guys out in five minutes or less. When I entered the room four older Lineman sat on the panel, along with the director Bob Bass sitting adjacent to them to the far right of me. I shook their hands, smiled and took a seat. As I sat there my heart began to pump and I felt my deodorant began to fail as the cold sweat streamed down my underarm. My future was staring right at me. In the first minute they went through my paperwork, noting my grades and climbing pictures; never once did they look at me. After a few grumbles one of the men asked what kind of experience did I have? When I began to address this concern, another cut me off mid-sentence and asked what I was doing before I applied for the position, since I didn't have much of a job history. Time stopped for a split second as I went straight from the heart with my response.

"I was in prison for six years because of poor choices, but while incarcerated I wrote a book, exercised, and studied electricity. When I paroled, I enrolled into college to further my study of electricity. Now I work making money to pay for my class A license."

While I was talking, they all looked up from what they were doing and listened to me. I let them know that all I had been through up to this point had prepared me to be an apprentice Lineman. The room went silent for a minute as these men looked me in my eyes nodding their heads in approval. The presence of God was felt that day by me in that moment. Shortly after the interview was over and they informed me that I would be hearing from them within a week with a score.

The way the system is set up at the JATC for interviewing is the lower your number the better chance you must get in or you can get immediately indentured into the program with no score. However, this rarely happened, especially with no experience or class A licenses; I only had a permit at the time of the interview. A week went by and a letter from the JATC was waiting on me when I got home from work. I closed the mailbox and walked home clutching the letter like it was a winning lottery ticket. Once inside the house I sat down at the kitchen table and opened the letter. It stated that I had immediate indenture into the program and would be starting a week from the mailing date. To describe the emotion and feeling would be hard. I was overwhelmed and thrilled to see all my hard work pay off; I experienced another surreal moment right there at my kitchen table. While I was ecstatic, it was short lived because I knew this was only the beginning of my journey.

In my opinion it is great to savor the victory, but foolish to relish in it too long because you start to quell the hunger that garnered the first victory. It's prudent to always reset yourself for the next victory and it's far easier to keep consistency during these times because momentum is hard to gather from a still position. After giving my notice to Sleep Train I started to go climbing every day after work on the poles near my house. It had been over a year since I touched the wood and I needed to refresh.

The first day of climbing class, which was part of the apprenticeship, I was there before the sun rose ready to work, when the doors opened an hour later twenty-five guys in FR shirts and jeans filed into the classroom ready to endure the Riverside heat. The first few days doing up-downs on 45 ft. poles in mid-July were brutal and its event sent a few guys to the hospital. At the end of the two weeks the core class remained. At the end of the two weeks we all received our job dispatch to different areas within California.

My first job as a first-step apprentice was in El Central California doing transmission for PAR.

For a second, imagine your first few weeks as a baby. Unable to formulate your thoughts or motor functions, you were utterly vulnerable in a world of chaos, yet you possessed survival instincts at the highest level communicating with your screams to be heard.

As an adult trying to find your way after being locked away physically and mentally, your biggest strength is your vulnerability. Embrace this and take to new endeavors with the vigor of a child trying to survive taking every lesson life brings your way. Find a fire in molding mistakes and success together to bring you closer to your goal. Do not allow setbacks to deter you from succeeding.

Up until working for PAR I thought line work only consisted of climbing poles and energizing power lines. I was unaware of the many avenues that went with the trade, like constructing towers, rail work, and underground. Yet my mentality was to succeed no matter what was set before me; so, there I was with no idea of what was going on around me. I'd never done construction before and lacked mechanical skills as well as a mechanical mind to see the big picture regarding the job. What I did have though, which I had from my days in the street and was invaluable? Heart. You can't undermine your traits at all. If you can breathe you can accomplish whatever you put your mind to. Climbing those towers, the first few days hurt my body in ways I can't explain as I tried my best to show I wanted to be there in the extreme heat of the desert. My first crew was with Clint, a no-nonsense foreman, two Journeyman Lineman, and another apprentice Kyle and our groundman Joey. Our job was to do quality control on the steel structures, which consisted of checking towers to make sure they were built to code.

I stayed with that crew two weeks before I got transferred to another crew doing the same type of work, but at night. For the first few weeks I kind of floated around gathering that no one really knew what was going on. Looking back on it, I now realize how completely unorganized it was.

A lesson you can glean from this is that things are not always going to be black and white in the work field, but you must be centered to learn all you can of what works and doesn't work. Sitting and complaining about things out of your control will not solve them. You must not allow yourself to be overwhelmed by these situations because they are fleeting in the scheme of things. Furthermore, they will make you appreciate a system that works and respect what it took to make things run smoothly.

Welcome to life my friend, where things are not always fair. I was at PAR less than a month before I was fired by a racist foreman who I'd been warned about by others. Up until that point I had never experienced racism on a personal level, but at twenty-eight years old I was being fired for lack of production from a guy that sat in his truck the entire time, unable to read the prints to construct the structures we were building. In fact, he was a foreman by default because there was no one else to take the position. It took everything in me not to knock this dude down. This guy smiled in my face every day and knew I had a family to feed, but still pulled the trigger to derail my career as a first-step apprentice.

Instead of allowing this clown to win I used his attempt to fuel my success even more by analyzing what I could have done better. I was now aware of the traps that were before me. I knew I had to be the best Journey Lineman possible to prevent this action from happening to another. Often in these situations we are taught to protest and sue, but that rarely solves the problem. Most people don't care and often you will be ostracized and made to feel it was your fault; so, the best recourse is to become better and prove them wrong with a strong work ethic. Trust me hard work and knowledge triumphs all the time. Crying and complaining only garners fake understanding and empathy because successful people - no matter the color of their skin - can only relate to success; your cries will fall on deaf ears. In short no one cares about your problems, but you. Focus on how to succeed and build a solid reputation that supersedes you. If anyone tells you differently, they are pulling your chain and facilitating your failure for the future.

Life will go on despite your problems, believe me. It's your choice to move on with your life or be a constant victim. Escape from the mentality of telling people your sad story too often. I meet people who get off on reliving their past mistakes. Please, stop dwelling on the past and deal in the now. Allow yourself three minutes to vent if faced with opposition, then move forward. Don't forget that negative energy is real, and it will engulf you and spread throughout your life just like positive energy. It cannot be stressed enough that your thoughts will create your world.

After being fired from PAR I was dispatched to San Francisco to work on light rail. In my short time at PAR I managed to save a lot of money and always lived below my means. So, I took to this new assignment with the same vigor as I loaded up my Dodge Neon with all my tools. Driving up the coast was a freeing feeling. Besides trips to Las Vegas to sell drugs, I'd never really traveled before I went away to prison. I was unaware how expensive it would be until I arrived. The hotels in EL Central were $250 a week, while the hotels in San Francisco were close to $500 a week or more. I arrived on a Sunday and knew I would have to find shelter fast so that I wouldn't go broke. I paid the $75 at a local hotel for one night on the outskirts of San Francisco. In the morning I packed all my belongings and headed to work for my first day at a small company named Reliance Engineering. Our job was to work on a new light rail system that would be going through downtown San Francisco.

The first day all I did was stack parts for future jobs in the warehouse. This was great because it allowed me to search for housing after work. Luckily, I found housing with an Italian family for $550 a month on Craigslist. I had a good time in San Francisco and learned a lot in the short amount of time I was there, before being fired for stealing the owner's wallet. My crew had worked a good portion of the day doing light rail work in downtown San Francisco and we were preparing to head home when my foreman received a call that a night job had just been set up for us later that night and we shouldn't venture too far because we needed to be back in a couple of hours to set up for the night outage. So instead of going home we played tourist around Frisco. When we came back to the yard later that evening our General Foreman approached us all saying he needed to talk about a situation that had taken place earlier and that's when he confronted us about the wallet coming up missing. He started with a line from Pinocchio saying let your conscience be your guide and just admit who stole the money out the wallet. My first reaction was look at the cameras. No response was given just a blank stare from the GF and by the end of the night I had my termination slip in my hand. Less than a year into my apprenticeship I had been fired twice, which meant I now had to go before the committee to see what was going on with me. Embarrassment would've been an understatement. I felt lost at this point in my life, but I knew I would make it through because I knew my truth. Always do your best in all you do, and no one can take your truth from you.

I held my head high in front of that committee, despite the blame being put on me concerning my latest firing. Like I mentioned earlier, no one cares about your problems but, rather, how you intend to do better. It's in these situations that you must draw from your inner strengths and beliefs to abate tearing yourself or others down. Always be present in the "now" to find solutions to problems that arise in your life.

With two firings under my belt the apprenticeship committee was seeing a trend and made it clear that one more firing and I could be released from my apprenticeship. My next dispatch would be to Wilson Construction in Duarte. By this time, I was aware that every contractor had a culture and energy they were known for. Most contractors had cliques and a racist undertone to how they treated non-white employees. For the record, this isn't just in the line trade, it's prevalent in any and every industry. Be aware of the cultures that exist in your work arena and adjust accordingly. Another great tip is to seek out those at your company that have the same vibe as you and pick their minds on what you need to do to succeed and who you should avoid.

As you're probably aware, some gangs are known for violence, while others may be known for getting money and women. The same can be said for companies, schools, or any institution. You must know who you're dealing with and what matters most to them in order to win the game you're playing.

Despite all these tribulations coming my way, the hunger in me was still growing. I just needed a place to showcase my abilities and Wilson became that place. I stayed there for sixteen months and during that time I found both my confidence, experience and knowledge growing by leaps and bounds because of those (including myself) who took the time to teach and push me while learning from my mistakes.

My first day there I saw the truck of the foreman who fired me from PAR. I had gone an entire year without speaking to this person, who would never even give me the decency to look me in the eyes. Three months before leaving Wilson they merged crews as the project was coming to an end and one of the guys, they put on my crew was the infamous foreman. I looked up to the sky like *"Really God this what we are doing?"*. I laughed inside and thought this must be a test, especially when my new foreman introduced him to me and said, "Will is good; he will give you a hand on whatever you need." Later that week, while chilling at home on a Sunday, Charles Stanley came on the TV and preached a sermon on forgiveness. In that moment I was convicted and knew I was going to forgive this cat. It's weird to describe or explain, but in my heart, I knew I had to let go of the hatred I felt for this person. The decision to let the hate go was not for him, but me, as it allowed me to grow and be a better person. Allowing anyone else the authority over your life or decisions, always takes your eyes off the goal. I knew I had to release his grip over the place I'd held onto out of resentment, anger and bitterness. As soon as I did, I felt free.

Nothing changed about how I viewed the foreman, but I knew that at the end of the day they knew they were wrong for what they'd done; I didn't have to tell them that. I'd learned a while ago that an idiot is going to be an idiot and you don't have to be the one to give them their issue; let your work speak for you.

After Wilson, I went on to a few other contractors before going to Asplundh for a year doing distribution. I finished my apprenticeship at Henkel's and McCoy, where I am currently employed.

In closing you have gleaned that getting a job is easy, but maintaining it is a skill you must acquire. Truthfully, this is the only difference between successful people and non-successful people. Your race, beliefs, and gender will play a factor in how you are treated in the work environment - there's very little to get around that. So now that we have established that what will you do about it? Will you let this hinder you and your future family from living the life you know should be yours? Or will use my examples to look within yourself to become the success story that lies within you? Tapping into the testimony, while overlooking the factors that can play against you, is a small price to pay for financial freedom and enjoyment of life. Trust me I'm so glad I didn't give up or into the stereotypes placed upon me.

Life is good, and it can be good for you too!

Chapter 5
Living Below Your Means

When you grow up without wealth there is a strong desire to possess money and material things to gain respect from other people. Let's face it, all these things have been painted and shoved down our throats as having the ability to hand-deliver happiness to your door. It's the norm for those who grew up without money to want money and things that they were denied as a child; that desire only increases as we become older and attach these wants to our self-esteem. The more money we have the better we feel, the type of vehicle we drive the better we feel, and here lies the problem. You see, things like cars and clothes and money are external and fleeting, leaving us constantly in shambles as we tie our self-worth to them.

From my experience the only way to break this cycle of having a poverty mentality is to devalue these things and realize they are only as valuable as the worth you place on them. Remember: you are the true prize and the knowledge, spirit, and hustle you have been priceless. This is the true meaning of securing the bag.

Money is merely an object made to perform a task, not much different than a hammer. The sooner you realize and accept this, the sooner you'll be able to make your money work for you over time. Always use it for its purpose, which is to build a better life for you and your family. For instance, owning a home. For many, the idea of owning a home seems far-fetched and unattainable. The fact? We all have the resources to make the dream a reality. The first step to becoming a homeowner instead of a lifetime renter starts with how you prioritize things in your life. The first few steps include:

1. You need job history at least two to five years.
2. Fix your credit, if necessary. Attain good credit - the higher the better (700 and above) before you make any huge purchases.
3. Make sure you have a good - or great - source of income.

The purpose of this book is to switch your way of thinking in terms of how you view making a living along with life in general. To acquire property, you must have a career that will provide you with disposable income, so (in California) you want to be bringing in at least $10,000 a month after taxes.

To build your credit, if you need (not want) to buy things, make sure that you pay them off immediately. Depending on whether you use it to your advantage or irresponsibly, generally using credit is bad because it can give you a false sense of wealth and develop bad spending habits. As I've echoed earlier, you must play the game to get loans so be smart about it.

Purchase things that are congruent with your career like tools, materials, vehicles, work clothes, dental work. This is exactly how I built my credit when I got out of prison. Once you have your score where you want it to be, do not use your cards anymore and pay for everything with cash. From that moment on, your credit card should strictly be used for emergency purposes and not for leisure.

Another trap I see people fall into often is useless titles and degrees, neither of which will bring them immediate wealth. Outside of being a physician or practicing law, make sure the field you are pursuing in college is going to be worth the student loans you will acquire. You can't learn hustle from college; if that were the case there wouldn't be so many stories of struggling college graduates. You can only learn how money works by getting experience in the real world. Another trap I see people fall into is staying in school too long to avoid getting into the real world. Don't let college trap you by adding more classes on top of classes to make your degree better. Like swimming after training, there's no better teacher than jumping in and putting everything you've learned to work.

Lastly, get a mentor in the field you're interested in so that they can guide you and mentor you. There's nothing worse than making useless decisions, which waste money and time. If someone wiser and older has seen it all and been through it all, allow them to help guide you around those landmines.

Degrees in art, communications, social work will likely leave you broke and that's just real talk. There'll always be a need for labor, medical, and technology; anything outside of that, you should be prepared to struggle, unless you have a designated path and position in mind to accompany your major. However, if you're just taking these subjects because you're excited to tell people you're in college...you're only playing yourself. It's time to get real. Fast.

For the record, in no way I am bashing these careers or the people who have chosen to take them up for a profession. Yes, without a doubt, we need these fields in our society for it to function correctly. Because every person has different needs and goals in life, we must keep an open mind as to which career avenue will afford us the opportunity to achieve them. Some people don't want a family, others want a large one, some want to buy a big house and others want to live abroad and not be tied to anything. Still, if you're wanting more out of life, be cautious of pursuing majors that don't traditionally yield the opportunities needed to succeed on the level you need to succeed to live the life of your dreams.

So how does this all tie into living below your means? Simple, your career choice will greatly affect how you can save, budget, or set financial goals. In terms of income, you always want to cut things in half; what that means is when you see a salary posted always slice it in half to set your expectations. Let's say the company is saying a starting salary of $100,000 a year you want to cut that in half to see what you will be bringing home. So, if you cut that in half you now have $50,000 a year. Now, you want to divide that by twelve which brings you about $4,000 a month. If you are living in California rent can range from $800 to $1500 for a one-bedroom (depending on the area). If you plan on purchasing a new vehicle you are looking at a car note $300 to $800 (depending on your credit score), not to mention car insurance, which can range $300 to $500 a month. Finally, your fluctuating bills like utilities, emergencies, food, debt, and entertainment must be taken into consideration.

So, let's do the math hypothetically to see what the numbers come out to.

1.) $1500 for rent. If you are making $100,000 a year, you are probably going to want to stay in a decent area so plan on your rent plus deposit being high.

2.) $500 for your car note. Once again if you are making $100,000 a year you probably want a decent and reliable car.

1) $500 for full coverage car insurance.

2) $500 for miscellaneous bills and debt.

That means that $3,000 a month is needed (at a basic level) to survive the life you want to live.

In this scenario, this leaves $1,000 for the month and this is being generous. If you have children, that's another cost and another factor. If this person was to set a tight budget, they could save about $10,000 to $12,000 a year when you add bonuses and overtime hours. So, to purchase a decent house it would take them about three years when you factor down payments, closing costs, and reserve funds in their account for emergencies.

So, you can see how this income leaves this person tight financially with little wiggle room. You don't want to be in this situation because it is a recipe for disaster. Now, just imagine this same scenario with a person making the $20,000 to $50,000 per month income range. Got it?

Pride comes before the fall is such a true statement and I'm a living witness and victim of it. So, instead of going directly to rent a place when you first start working, consider renting a room or getting a roommate to reduce cost. Not only will that bring you to a decent monthly rent rate each month, but you'll be one step closer to ownership. Additionally, instead of buying a new car always stay moderate with something you can pay off quickly and really get value out of. I'd recommend places like CarMax, which help you stay away from lemons and keep you within your budget. Remember that a good solid car off the lot should run you about $10,000 to $13,000. If it seems too good to be true…well, you know the rest.

These are just a few examples of what you can do to see how much money you're going to need to make to get to your goals. Too often people hear that job brings in a $100,000 a year and they get excited without factoring in taxes. So now that you have a template you can accurately figure out a plan that will work for you and put you in the best position to win.

As we close out, keep these pointers in mind when financial planning.

Cars- It's better to buy a reliable vehicle for a few thousands than to get a car note, which will suck up a large portion of your income every month.

Career Fields- Do your research and get properly informed about the field you are going to invest your time into. Make sure you'll be making enough to get you to your goals as soon as possible. In the back of this chapter I have created a chart to give you an idea of how much you make an hourly accumulates in a day, week, month, and year to better give you an idea on how you will have to budget according to what you are bringing home.

Investment Properties - Consider getting an investment property before buying a home. This will serve as extra income and educate you on how to purchase more properties in the future.

Even Superheroes Need Help Sometimes

Be a Blessing - The most important aspect of living below your means is so that you can be a blessing to others in need. If you put others first, you will continue to win.

SALARY	DAY	WEEK	MONTHLY	YEAR
$10	$80	$400	$1,600	$19,200
$12	$96	$480	$1,920	$23,040
$15	$120	$600	$2,400	$28,800
$20	$160	$800	$3,200	$38,400
$30	$240	$1,200	$4,800	$57,600
$40	$320	$1,600	$6,400	$76,800
$50	$400	$2,000	$8,000	$96,000
$60	$480	$2,400	$9,600	$115,200
$70	$560	$2,800	$11,200	$134,400
$80	$640	$3,200	$12,800	$153,600
$90	$720	$3,600	$14,400	$172,800
$100	$800	$4000	$16,000	$192,000
$110	$880	$4,400	$17,600	$211,200
$120	$960	$4,800	$19,200	$230,400
$130	$1,040	$5,200	$20,800	$249,600

This chart is based on a forty- hour work week. Keep in mind bonuses, over time, time and a half, weekend work, and per diem can drastically affect the pay scale as well.

Chapter 6
The Company You Keep

Hypothetically, you've read this far and have started to apply the principles to your current life and situation. You've checked into a trade school of some sort or reassessed the direction of your career choice and are making better choices. During it all you are saying to yourself it's hard, but it's working how Will said it would.

Fast forward to five or 10 years later and visualize yourself making money and stacking it with not much time for anything else. Work and sleep are now your routine as everything else that was once appealing no longer has its shine. You're focused. Years in and your paper is strong and you're looking to purchase a new investment property. As you head to get a loan for your first purchase, you're surprised at how easy it is with good income and great credit.

At this point, having money is no longer an anomaly to you, it's rather routine...so now what?

Now you reconstruct your friendships, which should be easy at this point because those who really had your back are still around building too, while those who weren't as serious have now departed from your life. It's at this moment you must start finding people who are better off than you and seek guidance on how to take it to the next level. One thing to steer clear of are the fast-talkers and get rich overnight schemes. More likely than not, you are already better off than they are, and they know this, so they will try to entice you with slick words, promises and ego boosts, all to get your money. When these individuals approach you always question them about what they do. If they can't tell you directly what their business is, avoid them. For instance, you're now a homeowner so why would you take financial advice from someone who doesn't own a home? Secondly, don't be fooled by the flashy suits and luxury cars. Most of the time, these people get these vehicles from auctions and they have crazy high mileage on them; it's all a facade to appear like they are doing better than they truly are. Always stick with the facts when it comes to future investments and accept nothing else for yourself.

This way of thinking also applies when picking a mate. You should be questioning any potential mate or partner.

Questions like:

1.) What is their credit score? This will tell you if they have good decision-making skills.

2.) What's their family situation? This will tell you how they approach life.

Remember you are choosing to bring this person into your world, and they can either improve your situation are damage it. I'm not saying look down on anyone, but you must make sure that whoever you plan to build with shares your same goals. I've seen too many people make partner decisions based off superficial things like good sex, body parts, and looks (myself included) and it always ends badly in the long run.

For the ladies: marry before you carry. Period. Don't allow a man to impregnate you before he has married you. Simply put you are setting yourself up for a struggle. If a man truly values, you he'll want to give you that title instead of just a baby momma title and if he is unwilling to do that you must be willing to walk away from him. Wasting your time in directionless relationships will only set into motion a life of struggle, poverty, and heartache. Know your worth, know your importance and, most importantly, want greatness for all areas of your life.

Career development is only the first of many steps in building a great future you must also build a reliable support system too.

Chapter 7

Giving Back

I've learned that it's far better to be the giver than the receiver in life. Likewise, it's greater to be the one to be a blessing than the blessed. Having a heart to give will open so many doors for you as a person and that just doesn't mean financially. Too often we get caught up in the mindset that to give is solely currency-based, but that couldn't be more wrong. You can give your time, life experience, or skills to others even information.

Always work in your endeavors so that you can be a helping hand to another, and you will always be successful. You'll get out of life what you put in, and it's just that simple. If you put a half-heart into what you do, then everything will be equally repaid to you in return. You never know who is watching you and inspired by your walk. Too often we take ourselves for granted because we're not where we think we should be in life. Because of this, we go through life expecting things to be a certain way, which causes a string of let downs that we often self-create at times.

Life is growth and growth means thinking of how your actions will affect others. When you accomplish all your goals, you'll realize that a true sense of completeness is being a path for others to cross into their greatness.

In short, giving back can have many faces so….

Be a volunteer

Be a tutor

Be a counselor

Be a mentor

Be a parent

Be a partner

Be a friend

Be an encourager

Be an ear

Be a shoulder

Be a husband

Be a wife

Be yourself

Be great in all you do and to others

Be super in all you do!

www.ingramcontent.com/pod-product-compliance
Lightning Source LLC
Chambersburg PA
CBHW031207160426
43193CB00008B/533